GMC GUIDE

FROM SHIP TO SHORE

FEATURING THE THOUGHTS OF
KAUSHIK SEAL, AMIT KUMAR SHARMA, SONALI BANERJEE,
MOHIT KAPOOR AND OLYMPIA PAPAZOGLOU

GMC GUIDE

FROM SHIP TO SHORE

FEATURING THE THOUGHTS OF
KAUSHIK SEAL, AMIT KUMAR SHARMA, SONALI BANERJEE,
MOHIT KAPOOR AND OLYMPIA PAPAZOGLOU

DR BINAY SINGH

TWAGAA
HTTPS://TWAGAA.COM

TWAGAA
HTTPS://TWAGAA.COM

Mumbai (MH), India
Website: https://twagaa.com
Email: hello@twagaa.com

First published by TWAGAA INTERNATIONAL 2021

Title: GMC Guide - From Ship to Shore

ISBN: 978-93-91254-53-7

First Edition
Published in India

Ordering Information:
Quantity sales: Special discounts are available on quantity purchases by corporations, associations, and others. For details, contact the publisher at the address or email above.

ACKNOWLEDGEMENTS

We dedicate this book to all seafarers and maritime professionals around the world. Because of you, the world has made it through one catastrophe after another. We know that you will continue to work tirelessly, either at sea or on shore, and you can trust us to do the same.

Special thanks go to all the founding members of the Global Maritime Commmittee (GMC), Kaushik Seal, Amit Kumar Sharma, Sonali Banerjee, Mohit Kapoor, and Olympia Papazoglou, for sharing their inspiring real-experiences.

FOREWORD

Dr. Binay has always carved his path in the maritime industry in his own unique way. For a person of Indian origin, starting a maritime business in Ukraine and making it into a very successful company is unique and inspiring. He personifies 'Anything is possible if one sets a goal and works hard to achieve it.'

This book is addressing a very important need in the industry.

Most seafarers, at some stage, do think about 'coming ashore'. The reasons may be family, a desire to grow in the maritime industry, or the pursuit of setting up a business. There is not much information available to a seafarer on the opportunities, pathways, and challenges in making that transition.

This book addresses all the issues in a simple and conversational, easy-to-comprehend way.

The personal stories of seafarers who have successfully

made the transition are encouraging for anyone embarking on the journey of coming ashore.

I thank Dr. Binay for guiding and encouraging the seafarers to make the transition.

Wishing him great success.

Capt. Pradeep Chawla
MD - QHSE - Anglo-Eastern

CONTENTS

THE FIRST CONSIDERATIONS

When you first join your maritime academy, wide-eyed and optimistic, you dream of a life spent on the sea. You imagine all the adventures that you will find and the strange locations that you will encounter. It seems as if the rush will be too much. Even if it *does* never get to be too much, though, you may experience a change of heart at some point in your life. You imagine what your life could be if you were to take a different route. This does not mean that you regret pursuing a career in the maritime sector, only that you are thinking through all of your options. You are curious as to what other possibilities are out there – what more you can do in the maritime sector.

This is a *natural* shift for anyone. You begin your career as a seafarer, young and without any familial responsibilities. Then, things change. You decide that you would like to settle down and shift away from the on-the-go lifestyle that characterizes a career in maritime. A job in an office, which would have seemed distinctly undesirable when you were younger, begins to feel alluring, like the only thing that makes sense to you anymore.

There will be challenges, though. When you first entered maritime, you might have found yourself focused on a few key areas, the skills that you needed to develop and the career path that you needed to follow. When you are transitioning out of your role as a seafarer, from ship to shore, you have to ask yourself many questions that you have never asked yourself before. Let's look through some of those questions together, as compiled graciously by Amit Kumar Sharma.

Do I have the capital that I need to launch a business?

Even if your idea is one of the most groundbreaking and intriguing ones, even if you have found an audience for your business, and even if you feel confident in your knowledge of maritime, you will not make it far at all unless you have put away the capital that you need. Without enough capital, you will run into one obstacle after another, unable to overcome them, struggling to make any sustained progress. Even the slightest dilemmas will rapidly morph into daunting challenges.

How do I decide on the right business after I move from ship to shore?

It is never going to be completely obvious where your greatest success is until you make actual moves to get there. Without putting forth the necessary effort, researching and looking into all of your options, you are bound to feel like you are in the middle of a giant mystery, trying to put together the clues but more lost than anything else. At some point, you have to trust the decision that you make and move forward even if you feel a little uncomfortable. Until then, it is going to feel stressful.

What if I decide that I would like to go back to sea at some later date?

This happens! Even if you have thought carefully through your decision to move from ship to shore, you may change your mind again later. You may decide that as confident as you were that you were doing the right thing then, your situation is different enough that you would prefer to backtrack. All that you can do is remind yourself that the same way you had developed the necessary skills to make a life at sea in the first place, you can do so again.

What if my certifications and my licenses go out of date? What if there are new licenses that I need to get?

You may find yourself stuck on all the legal obstacles that you have had to overcome. You will think about all the paperwork that you have had to complete and the processes that you have had to pass in order to get out to sea to begin with. All of that time and effort, if your licenses expire, will seem like they were for nothing. You will feel like you are under an all-new burden, struggling just to return to where you once were. Even though you need to work through those emotions on your own, and decide whether or not they are going to be overwhelming for you, it may comfort you to realize that other people *have* made the switch and then gone back, either earning their licenses again or making it back before their expirations.

What if life on shore is not for me at all?

You would not be the first maritime professional to realize that any life away from the sea is personally unfulfilling. This is a question that you and you alone can answer, and unfortunately, you may not be able to answer it until you make the leap. Before you have *tried* a life on shore, the doubt will remain. You will always wonder if you could have done more good, if you could have earned more income, and if you could have established yourself in a more enriching career. On the contrary, once you have tried both, you will be able to say *from experience* which one is best for you.

Will the competition of the business world feel like too great of a weight for me?

Although seafaring is a uniquely challenging endeavor, it takes certain levels of finesse and fortitude to navigate entrepreneurship proficiently. Some people buckle under the weight of the competition. They see the rewards that the business world can yield – only to wind up emotionally drained as they try to fend off everyone else pursuing the *same* rewards. Even though nothing is permanent, and one failure does not mean that you are unfit for the business world, it is important to do some deep self-reflection so that you can decide whether or not it will become too much for you.

Each of these questions, especially if you have never considered them before, is important. The sea is a worthy environment for the most prodigious talents. If you feel like you belong there, like it is your home, then you need to respect that. You need to think slowly through this decision, proceed carefully through any transition from ship to shore. Many seafarers have left the sea, given up significant earnings, and then changed their minds. Others, however, have secured a lasting career on shore. They have felt happy and comfortable with the choices that they have made.

You never know *which* of these groups you are going to fall into until you have tried them both. Some people never feel like they *have* to try both. Others do. This is a determination that you need to make on your own, seeking out resources like those we provide at the Global Maritime Community (GMC), to inform your decision and to afford you the confidence you desire.

It is critical that you realize, for your own sake, that the greatest difficulties of a life at sea will never disappear. Seafarers, for all of the fulfillment and satisfaction that they get out of the work, also spend months at a time away from their families. Their schedules are not conducive to living much of a life elsewhere. Seafaring may, as well, cause emotional turmoil. When a seafarer is constantly thinking about life on shore, and all the comforts that it provides, he or she is likely to feel torn between that world and this one. An unsupportive company will only make the situation worse.

This is why seafarers so often seek out a move from the ship to the shore. It is not because they are thinking of the rewards that are possible through a career on shore – rewards that are substantial – but because the pressures of a life at sea have become too much for them. They start to feel unappreciated and uncompensated, viewing every difficult task as a slight against their character. The only possibility, it seems to them, is to do something different.

We must also consider another point: for seafarers whose only drive is to make money, a life at sea begins to seem more and more unattractive. They wonder if there is some other way, something easier and less stressful, some venture that they can pursue that does not put such immense pressure on their families. After conducting hundreds of interviews, we have found that among seafarers who want only to earn a lot of money, the potential for a career on shore is that much more feasible. They have simply never *thought* about anything else, considering that they could apply their skills to something outside of a ship.

We want to state upfront that our intention is neither to encourage nor discourage any maritime professional to go in one direction or another. What we want is for *each* maritime professional to decide for herself, to think through her options and figure out which of them will work in the long term. That could mean a life at sea for some, and it could mean a life on shore for others. There is no single answer that can or will work for everyone.

Remember this. Every person today, lives for around 70 years, depending on a range of variables, like gender, location, and dietary habits. Many live much shorter lives, 60 years or even 55. Even those who live 80 years, however, should know that there are limits on their time. In this beautiful world, each of us needs to decide what we are going to do – what is going to make us happy and what path is going to meet our needs the best.

This leads into the mission of the GMC: "Navigate your career, from ship to shore." We are providing seafarers and other maritime professionals a fuller, clearer, and more balanced picture of the lives that they have chosen. To those who have graduated from the maritime academy, we want to make it apparent that there are advantages and disadvantages to every choice. Nothing is going to be perfect, and no path is going to be objectively the best one. These are complex decisions, and to make them even *more* complex, they change based on the person making them *and* when the person is making them.

We at the GMC will, regardless of the complexity of these

choices, do all that we can to elucidate the most favorable possibilities to seafarers and other maritime professionals. Working tirelessly, striving endlessly, we will do our part to inform and educate. In this guide, you are going to get a firmer idea of what there is for you in maritime, as well as the points you may not have considered.

Happy sailing! (Or, enjoy your life on shore – whichever you choose.)

THE UNSEEN POSSIBILITIES

The truth about maritime is much deeper than what many people, even many industry insiders, seem to assume. Even though seafaring is a *huge* part of this industry, it is not the only job. Within maritime, there are entire teams of people who never go out to sea at all. Support staff, manning companies, and other teams do crucial work for the maritime sector, all without leaving their offices. They live lives that look no different than the lives that other office workers live.

None of this invalidates the anxiety you may be feeling about transitioning from ship to shore. If you are nervous, if you are uncertain, if you are hesitant to do anything at all, you should know that we empathize with you. We at the GMC have seen it all, have watched as people have spent years in at-sea roles they did not enjoy, all because the other possibilities intimidated them.

If this sounds like you, take a deep breath. Let's start by clearing your mind of all the assumptions that you may have made about maritime and any of the doubts that may have manifested themselves in your mind. We want to take an honest look at all your options, all the unseen possibilities in maritime, but we want to do so in a way that is *never* overwhelming. You should be able to make the leap, from ship to shore, without sending your mental health into a tailspin. The less reasonable a proposition sounds, the more useful all the information in this guide is going to be for you.

Think about the ships themselves. While they are at sea, the masters are in charge of them. That is the hierarchy – while they are at sea. Docked, however, the ships are the purview of shipping company managers. There are on-shore jobs for people who take responsibility for fleets. These jobs *still* come in direct contact with ships. If you have dreamed your whole life of working on a ship, you can do so, even without heading out to the sea for months at a stretch. There are many such jobs, all well-paying, all respectable.

There are also roles for those who work on behalf of other shipowners, maintaining the business of the ship while it is at sea. Maritime manning companies, such as the one that Dr. Binay Kumar Singh oversees, place seafarers on the ships where they can make the greatest impact. These companies play an integral role in keeping the maritime sector functional.

You may also, of course, go back to school and pick up some

skills for which the maritime sector is desperate. Take coding, for example. Because so much of the maritime sector has become dependent on technology, there is never a shortage of coding jobs. If you learn how to develop or maintain software, you can work behind a desk *and* remain in the maritime sector. You will be eligible for high-paying, stable jobs, all because of the new skill that you have picked up.

Perhaps you would like to put yourself on the *other* side of education. At maritime academies, colleges, and universities, you can pass your maritime skills, knowledge, and insights to the next generation. Young seafarers enter the maritime sector every single year, and before they can get onto a ship, they need to learn from someone who has already been there. Your transition from ship to shore may entail *teaching*, taking on a role as a lecturer or professor. These roles are particularly rewarding because you know that you are building the future of the maritime sector.

Say that, on the other hand, none of these roles sound attractive to you because you cannot stand to think of leaving ships behind forever. While you would like to spend much less time on the water, you imagine how demoralized you would feel to move on from that part of yourself. In that case, you may want to take a look at ports, where there are many jobs onboard ships – while the ships are docked. Surveyors, mechanics, and engineers all work on ships, and they only go out to sea for *pleasure*.

One of the first things that you need to consider, before you start to make your transition from ship to shore, is what you would like to get out of your career. Think about *why* you go to work at all, without using the word "money." You need to look at yourself closely, reflecting on the drives and motivations that have kept you showing up for each of the roles that you have taken on. There is something about maritime that has called you. In your new, on-shore role, the *same thing*, or something equally alluring, should be calling you. You do not want to make a transition only to realize that you regret the move. Even though you *can* backtrack, and change your mind, it is much easier to feel *great* about your choice the first time around.

If the challenge and the adventure of seafaring keep your heart pounding, then a life on shore will seem boring. Your transition, because of all that you are giving up, will wear on you. You will feel like there is something missing. Worst of all, you may blame yourself. You may conclude that there is something wrong with you, that it is because of some fault in your character that you have not been able to accept the choice that you have made.

That is never the case, though. There is nothing wrong with you, whatever decision you make and however you feel about that decision. On the contrary, if your transition is difficult, it is because there is something that you are missing. Emotions are always messages that we send to ourselves: if you are feeling negative emotions about your switch from ship to shore, then you need to pay attention to those emotions and decipher them. Ask yourself what you are trying to tell yourself and how it can inform the direction that your maritime career takes from this point forward.

Another unseen possibility is that you have not prepared for your transition adequately. For example, if you are pursuing a career in software development in the maritime sector, then you should look through the certifications and licenses that you will need. Fail to do that and you may not be able to find any work at all. Unless you have followed the steps that *everyone* in your position has to follow, you will run into trouble. Even worse, you will be running into trouble during an already stressful time of your life. You may start to feel like there is nothing you can do to correct your course at all, letting discouragement take over and make your decisions for you.

Know this: if you aspire to a managerial or senior role on shore, your seafaring education will not suffice. The credentials that you have used to get onto a ship may not, it turns out, be enough to get you off of it. To take on the most prestigious leadership roles, you need to earn an undergraduate degree and perhaps a postgraduate degree. These requirements will vary from role to role and from company to company. Once again, the answer is to do your research *before* you take any drastic steps. Until you can explain to someone else, in detail, what your dream job requires, you need to *keep exploring*.

Of course, we also need to consider the possibility that you have done everything you need to do, a life on shore is perfect for you, and you are about to make the best transition of your life. That is another possibility, and if you feel *comfortable* with your life at sea, then it may go unseen. Complacency should not, any more than any other negative emotion, guide you as you make this decision. You need to make a choice from your boldest and most courageous mindset. Ask yourself how you would like others to remember you, as a success on shore or as a success at sea, and then work from there.

It would be impossible for us to prescribe a thought process for *every* seafarer and maritime professional to follow. These are points and possibilities that you need to look through on your own. You need to consider all the work that you have done to get where you are, as well as the work that you will have to do, to reach an *ideal career*, something that works for yourself and for your family. While we can present you with tips and caveats, the choice will be yours.

There are, at the same time, challenges that are exceedingly common, if not almost universal. You may not be able to foresee every challenge that is ahead of you, but in the next section, we will talk about some of the ones you are most likely to encounter. The point is not to scare you or to discourage you from one choice or another, but to *prepare* you.

THE UNSEEN DIFFICULTIES

Think about this. If you were to pick up your whole life tomorrow, and leave behind everyone and everything that you knew, it would be a stressful experience for you. You would cycle through a range of emotions, none of them too pleasant. It would be a *culture* shock. When you switch from ship to shore, you can expect the same thing to happen. You are giving something up and making a change.

Difficulties are *impossible* to avoid.

Yet, we can deal with them. Even in something as basic as the atmosphere of your work environment, you will feel some stress. It will seem as if nothing is as you have known it to be. You will feel lost at times, confused at others, and frustrated more often than not. The pace of your work will seem to drag, compared to the excitement of life on a ship. Whereas you may have once dreaded waking up in the middle of the night to take care of a task on a ship, you will *miss* that urgency. You will miss the rush that you have gotten out of life on a ship – compared to the nine-to-five doldrums that you feel when there is nothing else for you to do outside of your workday.

On a ship, as well, there is always a clear hierarchy. You

answer to your superiors, and your subordinates answer to you. There are orders, which denote undeniable expectations and a firm bar against which success and failure must be measured. While the same hierarchies may apply in an office, you are much less likely to feel like there is someone in charge all the time. The order and discipline tend to break down a little more, in favor of a collaborative environment composed of equals.

According to one survey, 30% of seafarers who transitioned from ship to shore when they were young tended to look for a way back. The culture shock was too great for them, not least of all because of the patience that their on-shore roles demanded of them. Everything that they had imagined of a life on shore, everything that they had disliked about a life on a ship, seemed to reverse as they realized that neither was perfect.

At the GMC, we have taken a one-on-one approach to these issues. We work with seafarers individually, to get to the root causes of the stress and doubt that they feel. Our goal is to determine what is going wrong in their transition and what we can do to make some corrections. We *never* apply any one-size-fits-all strategies, believing instead that when we treat seafarers as unique men and women, we are more effective at guiding them through their difficulties.

Sometimes, difficulties are straightforward enough that seafarers and maritime professionals just need to change some of their habits. They can look at their schedules and routines, as well as the assumptions that they have made about their work lives, to determine where they may be getting stuck. A strong support system may also prove beneficial, especially if the on-shore role seems lonely compared to the tightly knit crews on which they have served at sea.

There are times that junior-ranking seafarers will look to make a transition from ship to shore, only to realize that they have not yet accrued the experience that they need. Although they *may* feel ready to do something different, the cold reality is that they have not made themselves sufficiently valuable. They would do well to put off their transition for at least a year or two, while they learn the intricacies of maritime. Life on a ship, if they are already seeking out an exit, may not be right for them in the long term, but for now, they need to put in their hours and gain a little perspective.

Senior-ranking seafarers, on the contrary, may be able to

offer a wealth of maritime knowledge – but may lack the soft skills they need to work on shore. Because the social environments are so different between a ship and an office, men and women who have spent many years at sea may find that they struggle to relate to those who have been on shore for most of their lives. They need to adapt in a more abstract sense, picking up communication skills and leadership skills that are more applicable to the office environment.

For each of these groups, self-awareness is necessary. Seafarers need to recognize and acknowledge what rank they have attained and then decide, from there, how they are going to move into their new, on-shore roles. Change is a valuable thing, when seafarers approach it respectfully and judiciously. At the same time, when a seafarer rushes into any decision, even the right decision, he sets himself up for disaster.

Let's consider a specific example of a successful transition from ship to shore. When a deck officer has served for several years, he is likely to have developed significant navigational skills, cargo skills, and experience with navigational bridge equipment. He also understands how to read customs and port papers, perusing them rapidly to get the key points.

His skills, while they may at first seem specialized to a life at sea, will apply well to a *training role* on shore.

Think about all the seafarers who have not yet served as deck officers. They also need to learn navigational bridge equipment and customs and port papers. Even to *begin* serving as deck officers, they need to learn the ins and outs of these topics. There is no way for them to do that, other than to learn from someone who has been in that position. Any deck officer can, therefore, transition from ship to shore by becoming an educator. They can make themselves useful to the maritime sector by passing on their knowledge.

The same precept applies to a variety of on-ship roles, including:

- cargo surveyor on bulk carriers
- draft surveyor on bulk carriers
- cargo monitoring officer
- cargo planner on containers
- weather routing and data monitoring
- VTS traffic monitoring
- customs clearance
- ship suppliers
- bunker surveyor

- ship waste management
- port safety officer
- manning documentation
- SCTW documentations

Many seafarers served in two or even three of these roles while they were on board a ship. They have, thus, made themselves two or even three times more valuable to the maritime sector. Whenever a seafarer takes on additional duties, he is in essence creating more opportunities for himself. These skills only *sound* like difficulties, like specializations that require one to stay on a ship, until you realize that the next generation of seafarers will need them too. Then, they become forms of empowerment. Every skill becomes a precious piece of information, an insight that belongs in an academy or a college, where other seafarers can have access to them as well.

The reality is that for every seafarer who views a difficulty as a difficulty, there is another seafarer who will view it as an opportunity. This is another example of the deeply personalized manner in which every maritime professional must approach a move from ship to shore. There is no one answer, and there is no one perspective.

If we enhance the skills of seafarers in these operations related to port and shipping, turning experience into education, we can boost young seafarers' to plan their careers. Even that does not solve *all* of our problems, however. There will be other, more abstract complexities, which we will cover next.

COMPLEXITIES OF THE TRANSITION

Because the seafaring culture emphasizes hard work and results, seafarers often find little encouragement to continue their education. Although they develop valuable skills while they are on their ships, they almost never secure a secondary degree. Then, they remain invisible to the world outside of the ship. Their fellow seafarers respect them, even admire them, for their ability and willingness to carry out their duties, but to the rest of the world, they merely seem uneducated. It seems impossible for them to be able to impress the maritime professionals who have built businesses and established careers on shore.

The coronavirus pandemic has revealed the hazards that this culture presents to seafarers. Any time there are shutdowns in the maritime sector, and ships are not able to pass as easily from one port to another, remote work will become the norm. This is already happening on a large scale, generating previously unseen opportunities in the economy. For seafarers who have not earned undergraduate or graduate degrees, however, these opportunities will be out of reach.

In the future, as additional crises impose such conditions on the world, those who have earned a degree will be at an advantage. Seafarers who have never even considered going back to school or transitioning from ship to shore will, unfortunately, be at the whims of governments and Mother Nature. They can do nothing but hope that things continue to run smoothly, that none of the changes that take place will be too jarring for them to handle.

A seafarer's life is, it is worth noting, not especially conducive to higher education. Spending months away from shore, they can hardly keep up with a five-day course schedule for a semester, at least not in the traditional sense. At the GMC, we work hard to make educational opportunities more accessible to seafarers. Still, the ideal would be a shift *away* from a culture that values degrees over skills.

Until that happens, until a seismic shift forces people to rethink the value they place on higher education, seafarers may respond to the complexities of the transition by enhancing their soft skills. They can make themselves more valuable and more amenable to work on shore by learning about communication, leadership, creativity, entrepreneurship, and the supply chain. That way, they prepare themselves to take on the on-shore jobs that are most in demand in the maritime sector, not just falling in line with the cultural push to become a "bachelor" in this or a "master" in that.

None of this will eliminate one hard-to-accept fact: many on-shore professionals will write off seafarers from the get-go. They will make unfair assumptions and draw unreasonable conclusions to exclude seafarers from the most lucrative jobs. Seafarers are guilty of this behavior themselves, presuming themselves unworthy or unqualified for the most rewarding on-shore roles. They convince themselves that they would be incapable of doing work for which employers normally require a degree.

Most times, these presumptions and assumptions are false. Other times, they are not. For example, if a seafarer has used the same ship equipment for twenty years, he may not be aware of the ECDIS GPS or the AIS radar. He may not have picked up these skills because his ship owner did not require him to do so. In that case, the complexities of the transition are not so complex at all: he needs to hit the books and get back to learning, to modernize his skills so that they are more widely applicable.

Software development, programming languages, and

cutting-edge technology are other matters, entirely. They are difficult to learn even for those who have already spent years practicing them. For a seafarer who has worked on the same outdated equipment for multiple decades, they present a *special* type of complexity. Remember, of course, that the harder a skill is to develop, the rarer (and thus more valuable) it is going to be.

This complexity presents another opportunity for maritime professionals: to bridge the gap between technical experts and practical workers. Because miscommunication is so common between these two groups, maritime professionals can set themselves apart by knowing enough about each environment, the technology sector and the maritime sector, to act as a conduit between them. The professional is, this way, making it easier for developers to engineer superb tools and for seafarers to use those tools.

These are the hard-to-pin-down questions that entrepreneurs frequently tackle. If they seem mind-boggling to you, that is good: it means you *get them*. It is because these questions are so difficult to comprehend and answer that for those who do, fantastic spoils await. Anyone who is looking to make a transition from ship to shore, if she is brave enough to take on one of the most persistent and complicated challenges in the maritime sector, is likely to become an enviable success. Success is, afterall, not as uncommon as rain in the desert.

Next, let's talk about a few successful transitions from ship to shore.

SUCCESSFUL TRANSITIONS TO INSPIRE

When you are standing before a possible transition from sea to shore, you may feel isolated. You see all your peers heading out on another excursion, signing another contract to live at sea, and believe that there is no other way. When you think about the *possibility* of a transition from ship to shore, it fills you with anxiety. You imagine that no one has ever done such a thing before, at least not successfully. The more you think about your options, the more likely it seems that you *have* to stay at sea.

Too many seafarers, unfortunately, never get over this line of thinking. They go on in the same maritime roles for years. For one reason or another, they let discouragement overwhelm them. They decide that they are not even going to *look* at their other options. It is sad when this happens – and tragic if it happens long enough to take up an entire career.

To make yourself the exception, to pursue a switch from ship to shore and then *succeed*, you should consider those who have gone before you. Remind yourself that you are *not* the first to do this. You are not alone in your drive to think through all the possibilities for your career. If your entrepreneurial spirit seems to be tugging you a certain way, you are not alone.

Kaushik Seal, talking about his successful transition from ship to shore, says, "After my sailing stint with the Great Eastern Shipping and having sailed as a Chief Engineer, I decided to come ashore. So when I signed off from the vessel in August 1993, I was lucky to get an offer from Lloyd's Register as an Engineer Surveyor, which I gladly accepted. The rest, as they say, is history."

For him, the transition was smooth. Though, it might not have seemed that way at the time, to someone whose demeanor is neither as calm nor as strong as Kaushik's. It was because of his ability to see through the challenges that he was able to proceed through the transition easily and painlessly. Others, in his position, might have turned it into a thing of stress. They might have made the process more difficult for themselves than it had to be.

Olympia Pampazoglou, talking about her reasons for entering the maritime sector, also highlights an important lesson for all maritime professionals. She says, "I come from Greece, which is the number-one ship-owning nation in the world. The maritime industry offers a lot of opportunities and a really challenging environment to grow and get in touch with a lot of different nationalities and cultures."

Notice that she did not say *seafaring* specifically. Olympia says that *the maritime industry* offers "a lot of opportunities and a really challenging environment to grow and get in touch with a lot of different nationalities and cultures." Because of her optimism, she was never going to find any dearth of options on-shore. She was always going to see every possibility objectively, working through her career rationally and sensibly, leading to the most successful outcomes.

Asked what challenges he faced when he transitioned from ship to shore, Kaushik rattled off a list, "Adjusting to a 9-to-5 job, working with a lot of junior colleagues, not being used to local/domestic travel, not having the adequate skillset/ mindset for working ashore, and a lower salary and hence less savings."

It should feel *empowering* to hear that someone as successful as Kaushik has gone through such difficulties and come out *thriving* on the other side of them. His story is one of obstacles met and then overcome. To see him today, one may conclude that he has taken an easy path, that he has never felt the same doubt and hesitance that so many others do. His power comes, though, not in spite of the obstacles that he has met but *because* of them. As we say in Ukraine, smooth waters do not make fine seafarers.

Kaushik, going on about the timing of his transition from ship to shore, says, "When I was in the Marine University, I had decided not to sail for long after becoming a Chief Engineer, so I guess that plan was successful." It was, in this case, always the plan. He intended, from the beginning, to make the transition after he had achieved a certain title. Yet, for others, that is not the case.

Olympia, unlike Kaushik, made multiple attempts at pursuing her dream in maritime. She succeeded at transitioning to maritime entrepreneurship only on her third try. In her own words, "I made the transition a year ago, but I had made two unsuccessful attempts in the past. I always knew deep inside that one day I would become an entrepreneur. I am a leader and I have an innate creativity that needs to be channeled productively."

Her story should, as well, inspire those who are feeling

consternation about their transition. She listened to her instinct, paying attention to the message that her inner voice was sending to her, and it worked out. Three times over, she devoted herself to entrepreneurship. When others would have given up, she did not.

It is also worth mentioning that even among impressive successes like Olympia and Kaushik, a firm decision may entail some second-guessing. Asked whether he feels satisfied working on shore, Kaushik responded, "Yes indeed. Never regretted leaving the sea, although at times I have felt that the sea is calling me back, but I guess I resisted the temptation!"

Your experience will be your own. It may take you multiple attempts to reach your goals and to drive your greatest ambitions in the maritime sector. After a few setbacks, you may feel discouraged. Work through that feeling, and over time, there is no telling how far you can get. Years later, you may view your work at sea as a catapult to your passion, your seafaring days as mere precursors to the job that you perceive as your calling.

As long as you are true to yourself, success will follow. It will take time, of course, as all good things do. At the GMC, we are there to help seafarers and maritime professionals through the most grating and challenging times in their careers. We guide them as they manage their emotions and work through obstacles, unlike any they have encountered on a ship.

This is work that you can do for yourself, as well. Every step that you take toward making yourself more valuable, you prepare yourself for *more choice*. You may, as Kaushik has, feel the temptation to return to the sea *all your life*. Whether or not you listen to that temptation is up to you. The point is that you will be able to choose, not feel cajoled one way or the other.

Let's talk next about specific methods that you can use to make yourself more valuable as a maritime professional.

MAKING YOURSELF MORE VALUABLE

In the maritime sector, as in the rest of the economy, you are only as valuable as the use that you can offer to others. To earn a higher income, you need to be able to set yourself apart in the job market. As someone who has spent a great deal of time on board ships, you may feel like you are *far* less valuable than your on-shore competitors. You see how they navigate the office environment, and it all seems foreign to you. It seems unimaginable, to think that you could ever become as smooth or as comfortable as they seem to be.

If your aim is to make your transition from ship to shore successful, then you cannot let your self-doubt get in the way. At the same time, you cannot overlook the real deficits with which you are operating. There is a balance here: you need to present yourself confidently *yet* realize that there are skills you have not yet developed and insights you are not yet able to draw. As a seafarer, you have learned how to excel on ships, not on shore. Your skills will translate, but it will take some effort.

You *must* think about the real-world needs most common in the maritime sector. We at the GMC hear it again and again: seafarers, because they have not yet bought into their own value as maritime professionals, fail to communicate their value to others. They slog through interviews and networking events because, all their careers, they have relied on someone else to issue an order and tell them what they do. In this area, at least, you need to give *yourself* orders.

Mohit Kapoor, whose expertise is in marketing and public relations, has explained what maritime companies, and in turn maritime professionals can do to market themselves more effectively. He says, “There is a need for promoting the maritime industry as an adventurous and leading sector in terms of size; raising awareness, driving positive societal change, and demonstrating sustainable practices for future generations to get attracted to maritime sector; demonstrating other maritime segments like shipbuilding, repair, and recycling industry as major divisions of the maritime sector; and appointing brand ambassadors for promoting seafaring as a career.”

Each of those concepts, if you extrapolate them to your career in maritime, comes down to your willingness and your ability and to make your value *known*. On board a ship, you may count on your superiors to notice when you do your job well, but on shore, there will be no one to help you plead your case to potential clients, employers, and colleagues. *You* need to make yourself more valuable, by making your value apparent.

For women in the maritime sector, there are, of course, particular challenges. These challenges, like the challenges that all seafarers face in their transition from ship to shore, may seem insurmountable, at times. At the GMC, we are doing our part to support women. Sonali Banerjee, a thought leader on women in the maritime sector, puts it thus: "We can support women in maritime by creating a more inclusive environment and raising a greater level of awareness among the ship owners, to give women seafarers a more level playing field." As a woman, there is a critical opportunity there: *you* can make yourself more valuable by, in the way that Sonali is, taking a stand for other women. You can find ways to help them, just as she has.

Sonali goes on to say, "The selection process for women, just like for men, needs to be strengthened to identify those with the right mindset and attitude, to take up the seafaring profession." While this area may seem outside your control, you would do well to keep it in mind during your transition from ship to shore, remembering that employers, colleagues, and clients are *looking* for maritime professionals who have embraced values such as productivity and positivity.

Speaking to her own challenges in the maritime sector, Olympia says, “In this sector they require previous work experience which I did not have when I graduated from university, and finding my first job was tough. Another challenge was being a woman in this industry. I was continuously getting rejected from roles that I liked because companies preferred men.” Here too, you see the progression, from rejection to success, from denial to achievement. Olympia’s story, for women especially, should serve as motivation.

There was, as Olympia puts it, no direct path from where Olympia was to where she wanted to go – which was why she needed to carve out a path of her own. She says, “I had to leave my country Greece and work for a foreign company in order to have the chance to occupy the role I wanted. I started as a shipbuilding engineer/supervisor, then I grew to team leader and project manager. I have to say that in order to grow I had to pursue really challenging projects and change companies every two years.”

Your path too may be so unique that no one else has walked it yet. As a seafarer, you may find yourself surrounded by men who are content to stay in the same roles in which they have served for years. If your goals and your ambitions are different from theirs, then it may be difficult for you to relate to them. When you describe what you would like to do with your life, they either laugh or scowl. You need to remember, however, that your dreams are valid, as long as you pursue the education and the opportunities necessary to bring them to life.

The "how" will become much clearer to you once you start working on yourself. As you take one step toward making yourself more valuable in the maritime sector, other steps reveal themselves. You will realize that all along, the map that you needed has been inside yourself. It will take you to places you have never considered before. Keep following it, even when you feel nervous to do so. The transition from ship to shore will seem more and more plausible.

You will start to understand, on a deeper and deeper level how you can apply all your seafaring skills to your new work environment. Your office will feel more comfortable, and your obstacles will feel more quotidian.

Now, let's go over the longer-term details you need to consider as you transition from ship to shore.

RIDING THE WAVE TO THE FUTURE

In maritime, there is never a single pathway. You may begin on a ship and then remain there your whole life. On the other hand, you may spend one year on a ship, decide that it is not for you, and pursue a career on shore. You may feel your entrepreneurial juices flowing and launch your own business. The possibilities are more varied in maritime than in any other sector. Whatever you would like to do, you can do it here. The key is to remain open to the opportunities that appear in front of you.

Millennia old, the maritime sector permeates all our lives. Manufacturers in Southeast Asia ship their products via containers, and farmers in the Americas ship their produce the same way. On every shipment, every ship, there is a crew. More than that, there is support staff, remaining behind on shore. The support staff is responsible for everything except what the crew must do on the ship. From manning, the initial placements it entails, to finance, calculating costs and setting the prices, there are *more* on-shore roles in maritime than there are at sea.

This reality becomes more expansive all the time. Year after year, the maritime sector grows. Jobs that exist today did not exist last year, and on and on, the same will remain true. This is the only constant in maritime, the undeniable growth, and if you are looking to build a career somewhere, you may as well start at the foundation of the economy, the sector upon which every other sector depends. No crisis can shut it down, which is *wonderful* news for anyone most interested in job stability. Rest assured, we at the GMC will be there all the way through, for seafarers as well as other maritime professionals who have chosen to work on shore.

India, a developing economy, has already experienced some of the benefits of maritime, and it will continue to experience more. As Mohit explains, "Maritime in India will cater to environmental issues and emissions, the most significant technological drivers of change. Digitalization of ship operations will play a major role. Innovation in marine technology and changing dynamics of maritime business will help the Indian ship trade grow."

Think about each of those points: environmental protection, digitalization, ship trade. There are *many* more jobs on shore for these movements. While seafarers will remain employed, the opportunities on shore are undeniable. Anyone who *wants* to find a job on shore will be able to find two or three if he or she works with the proper mindset and thinks through options sensibly.

Even progress for women, who remain at a statistical disadvantage due to systemic misogyny, are doing better today than ever. Sonali says, "Taking up the theme of women in maritime in line with the UN SDGs, women have gotten a lot of visibility and prominence in the maritime industry. Some policy level changes were also incorporated to create space to induct women in the maritime industry and to make the industry more gender-sensitive. In India, definitely, the number of women undertaking maritime studies have gone up." She adds, however, "The percentage of women getting placed is still low."

The way that we see it, the work that we need to do is no reason for discouragement but for celebration. We feel *joyous* to realize that there is a purpose for all of us in the maritime sector. There is a calling for each of us, at sea or on shore, whichever we prefer. There is no reason for *anyone* to perceive limitations in maritime. Even if you are on the tail end of a thirty-year career at sea, you can try something else. You can choose to take a new path and try something different. All that begins with a touch of self-belief and a burst of motivation.

As soon as you have foreseen new possibilities, you can start the learning process. Educate yourself about the precise steps that others in your situation have taken. There are many role models and mentors accessible to you, if you go looking for them. Reach out to maritime professionals who have succeeded in their transition from ship to shore and ask them what challenges they faced and what advice they would offer you. What you will find is that most will be happy to help you. They will be glad to see that someone else is taking the leap, that someone else is risking it all on *themselves*.

Little by little, you will feel more at ease in your life on shore. You will look back on your time at sea as a grand adventure, one that you would have never given up but one that is firmly in your past. Spending more time with your family, living a more normal life, and taking none of the risks that a life at sea require, you will be able to tell your "seafaring stories" to your children, whom you get to watch grow up – because the days of six-month excursions and two weeks of shore leave have passed.

We at the GMC will be there to help you through anything that seems too unnerving. Here's how.

DOING OUR PART

We at the GMC believe that when they educate themselves, seafarers are some of the most efficacious and constructive professionals on the planet. Each of us has watched proudly as the maritime sector has remained on its seemingly incorrigible path toward historic highs, something of a quarterly event, so reliable is growth in the sector. We also know that there is room for improvement, though. That is why we have dedicated ourselves to *serving* the maritime sector. We want to make more seafarers aware that if they feel stuck or trapped at sea, there are other options within their reach.

This is not a flash-in-the-pan exercise for us. We are all *career* maritime professionals. Building our own thriving businesses, establishing ourselves as thought leaders, and networking internationally, we are demolishing the barriers that have – for too, too long – kept seafarers in place. The way that we see it, no seafarer should feel that there are any limits on his or her options. Every seafarer, whatever they would like to do with their lives, should feel capable of proceeding boldly.

Hollow inspiration is not going to do, though. To overcome past obstacles and to escape the momentum of "the way it's always been," we need seafarers to start to take responsibility for their own careers. There is a natural stodginess there, of course. We train seafarers to obey orders and to carry out their duties, not to think creatively or to question mainstream messaging. As a result, we are not doing everything we can to prepare them for more maverick careers, to point out the entrepreneurial spirit and tell them, "You can do that too."

Old habits, as the saying goes, do die hard. This is why we need to put *more effort* into shining a light on the transition from ship to shore. Even though it may not be the right choice for every seafarer, it is the right choice for many. Seafarers who feel dissatisfied, who would feel happier in a more normal lifestyle, end up faltering in their productivity – or worse. It is our joint responsibility to show them that there is hope, something outside of seafaring to which they can commit themselves.

This is how we are going to make the maritime sector stronger, through personal and individual effort. Wide-reaching programs may look fine on paper, but to make a real difference, we need to meet seafarers where they are and speak to them in a manner that they will understand. We need to make it clear that they can look beyond the careers that they have built, that they can seek out careers that feel *exciting* and *rewarding* to them.

Consider, for a moment, the size of the maritime sector. Currently, 90% of all goods wind up at their destinations because of ships. None of the major technological advancements in flight or in road transportation has been able to change that. Shipping, more than any other logistical means, is the basis of our economy. People live better when we all do better. They *count* on all of us to follow through on our promises, as well as to settle into roles in which we will be happy.

Maritime has, for all of the challenges that we can talk about, remained an affordable means of commerce too. This is only possible because of those at sea and those on shore working hand-in-hand. Without that collaboration, without their combined efforts, something like a bag of grain's price would *skyrocket*.

On every ship – tankers, passenger ships, container ships, fishing vessels, bulk carriers, and general cargo ships – there are men and women working hard. Behind them, there are on-shore maritime professionals, keeping the maritime firms running. We at the GMC salute both seafarers and maritime professionals equally. To them, we would like to deliver a clear message: we see you, and we are here for you.

Every day, we hear from seafarers who feel compelled to think about a life on shore. They are, for their own reasons, considering whether they should make a change. To them, it may seem as if such a change is tantamount to an overhaul of their whole lives. They identify with seafaring, as so many of us have at some point. Talking to them, you are not only talking to reason but to emotion, to the feelings that they have invested into maritime.

To us, there is always a rational argument in either direction, a reason to stay at sea, a reason to move to shore. These reasons convolute the topic. No one is entitled to say that one is better than the other, except the person who is *making* the transition. Knowledge, however, tends to make it more evident which is better, from one situation to the next.

We will continue, therefore, to provide knowledge wherever we can. When seafarers approach any of us, we will let them know what has worked in transitions from ship to shore and what has not. We will tell them our own success stories, how we have built businesses on shore, how we sometimes miss the sea. That is the only way to talk about any of this: telling the complete story, in all its gritty (and sometimes confusing) detail.

While you make your transition from ship to shore, try to simplify the discussion as much as you can, without eliminating anything that you need to consider. If that sounds challenging, *it is*. It has been challenging for many people throughout history. You fall in love with the sea, and thinking that you will never give it up, you let that love define you. Then, something else happens: the birth of a child, a new marriage, the death of a parent. Life nudges us in new directions, and all we can do is follow them.

Whenever you think through any change, especially a change from ship to shore, ask yourself *what you do not know*. Ask yourself also what you *believe* you know, but may not. As American novelist Mark Twain once said, "It ain't what you don't know that gets you into trouble. It's what you know for sure that just ain't so." You want to eliminate any ignorance as you think through this process. This is your life that you are planning, and it is worth taking extra care.

There is one thing that unites us, one thing that we all share in common: we are all passionate about learning. Business, maritime, or anything else, there is no end to the subjects that we study and share together. That is a motivation for all of us - to understand the world better, to solve its problems more fully. Because of that passion, that drive to *get it*, we feel confident when we need to make changes of our own. Out of doubt, we step into awareness. We *make* our decisions simple, by breaking them down into pieces and then analyzing the pieces against any information we can find.

You too, if you read and learn ferociously, will find that this decision, to stay on a ship or to settle in on shore, clears up much more quickly than it seemed possible. Keep learning, keep growing, and make the choice that is right for you.

ABOUT THE AUTHOR

Dr Binay Kumar Singh, Founder & CEO of *Singh Marine Management Ltd.* in Odessa (Ukraine) and Founder & President of *Federation of Global Maritime Community,* is an entrepreneur, author, and public speaker. His life mission is to serve the world's communities and guide everyone through positivity, love, and enthusiasm. This is reflected in his simple and timeless life philosophy: "Treat people as you like to be treated."

Dr Singh has a Master of Science in Marine Navigation and a Doctorate of Philosophy. He is a globally recognized expert in international shipping with over two decades of experience. Dr Singh is also taking wonderful measures for the needy community of the society as well. His new project with the name “Selfless Fund” is specifically targeted to help those who are in need. Dr Singh has also launched his new company GSR which is going to bring innovations to the shipping and maritime industry. His efforts for the shipping industry as well as for the society is an example of his generosity and selflessness.

He enjoys pursuing multiple passions like singing, dancing, playing the piano and the accordion, and keeping healthy by practicing yoga and CrossFit.

Email: binay@drbinaysingh.com
Website: https://drbinaysingh.com

MORE BOOKS BY DR BINAY SINGH

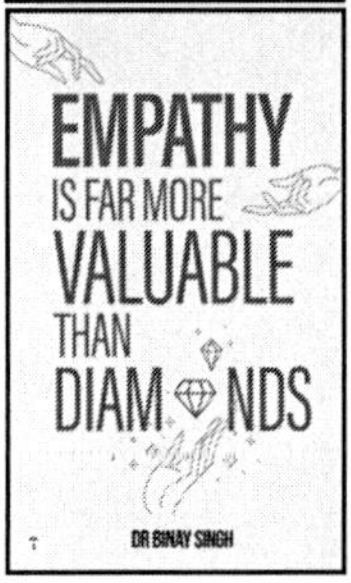

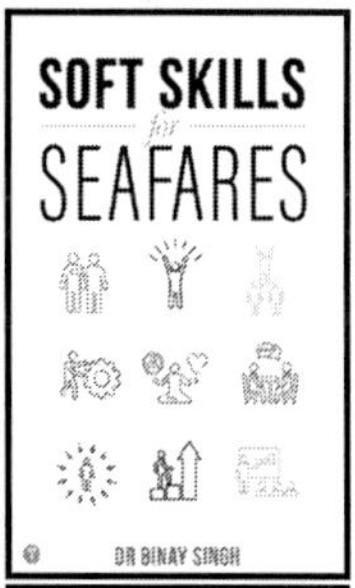

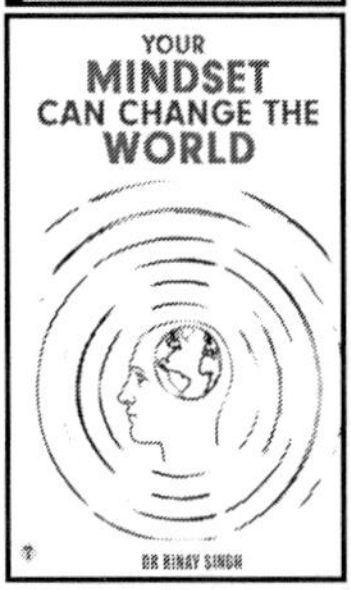

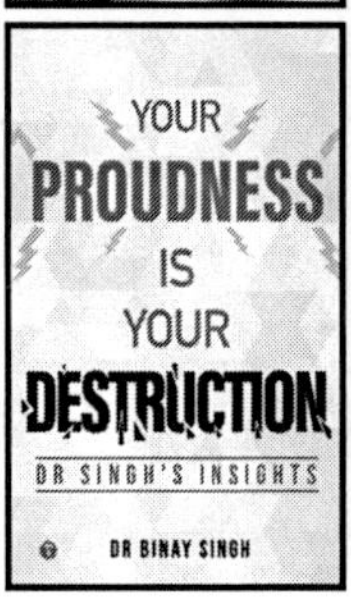

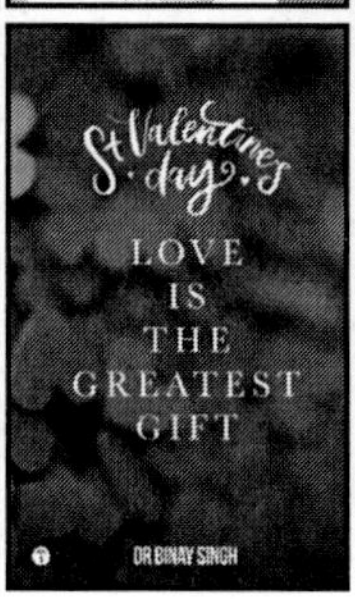

THE ART OF MARITIME MANNING
MY INSIGHTS
DR BINAY SINGH
THE ART OF NEGOTIATION
DR SINGH'S INSIGHTS
DR BINAY SINGH
THE ART OF SMARTPHONE-LIFE BALANCE
DR SINGH'S INSIGHTS
DR BINAY SINGH
ODESSA
MY CITY, MY HOME
DR BINAY SINGH
DIGITAL ADDICTION
KEEP YOURSELF AND YOUR FAMILY SAFE
DR BINAY SINGH
THE ART OF TEAM MANAGEMENT
DR SINGH'S INSIGHTS
DR BINAY SINGH
THE ART OF LEADERSHIP AT SEA
DR SINGH'S INSIGHTS
DR BINAY SINGH
SHIPS & RELATIONSHIPS
DR BINAY SINGH
MY FANTASTIC VOYAGE TO ODESSA
DR BINAY SINGH
THE ART OF GIVING
DR SINGH'S INSIGHTS
GIVE
DR BINAY SINGH
A MESSAGE TO YOUNG SEAFARERS
DR SINGH'S INSIGHTS
DR BINAY SINGH
Svetlana
DR BINAY SINGH
THE ART OF MOTIVATIONAL SPEAKING
DR SINGH'S INSIGHTS
DR BINAY SINGH
BE REALISTIC IN YOUR Expectations
DR BINAY SINGH
The TRUE MEANING OF HOPE
DR BINAY SINGH
AVOIDING DISTRACTIONS ACHIEVING SUCCESS
DR SINGH'S INSIGHTS
DR BINAY SINGH
THE ART OF TIME MANAGEMENT
DR SINGH'S INSIGHTS
DR BINAY SINGH
THE ART OF DISCIPLINE
DR SINGH'S INSIGHTS
DR BINAY SINGH
Care WITH YOUR WORDS
DR BINAY SINGH
MR POSITIVE
DR SINGH'S GUIDE TO LIVING YOUR BEST LIFE
THE Magic OF MUSIC
DR SINGH'S INSIGHTS
DR BINAY SINGH
DR SINGH'S GUIDE TO REAL HAPPINESS
DR BINAY SINGH
THE NEW MARITIME WAY
DR BINAY SINGH
DR SINGH'S GUIDE TO REAL SUCCESS
DR BINAY SINGH
THE NEW ERA OF BUSINESS TRAINING
DR BINAY SINGH